THE ULTIMATE
SCOTTISH SLANG
DICTIONARY

FROM "BRAW" (MEANING EXCELLENT) TO "DREICH" (DESCRIBING A DREARY DAY), THIS BOOK IS PACKED WITH OVER 250 LOCAL TERMS, FUNNY PHRASES, AND CULTURAL EXPRESSIONS THAT WILL HELP YOU:

- NAVIGATE SCOTLAND LIKE A LOCAL.

- IMPRESS FRIENDS WITH YOUR NEWFOUND SLANG SKILLS.

- UNDERSTAND THE HUMOR, HISTORY, AND HEART OF SCOTTISH CULTURE.

HELPFUL FOR TRAVELERS, LANGUAGE LOVERS, AND ANYONE WHO WANTS TO ADD A WEE BIT OF SCOTTISH FLAIR TO THEIR VOCABULARY!

Table of Contents

• Pronunciation Guide..Page 5

• Section 1: A to Z Scottish Slang Words and Expressions.......Page 9

A	Page 9	N	Page 45
B	Page 11	O	Page 47
C	Page 16	P	Page 48
D	Page 20	Q	Page 51
E	Page 24	R	Page 52
F	Page 25	S	Page 53
G	Page 28	T	Page 59
H	Page 34	U	Page 61
I	Page 37	V	Page 62
J	Page 38	W	Page 63
K	Page 39	X	Page 66
L	Page 40	Y	Page 67
M	Page 42	Z	Page 69

• Section 2: Scottish Phrases & Idioms.................................... Page 71

Scottish Slang Pronunciation Guide

1. The Scottish Alphabet

Letter	Pronunciation	Example
A	"Ah"	"Braw" (great) = "Brah"
B	"Beh"	"Bairn" (child) = "Beh-rn"
C	"Seh" (soft) or "Keh" (hard)	"Craic" (fun) = "Crack"
D	"Deh"	"Dreich" (dreary) = "Dree-ch"
E	"Eh"	"Ken" (know) = "Kehn"
F	"Feh"	"Faff" (mess around) = "Faff"
G	"Geh"	"Gie" (give) = "Gee"
H	"Hoh"	"Hogmanay" (New Year's Eve) = "Hoh-muh-nay"
I	"Eye"	"Aye" (yes) = "Eye"
J	"Jeh"	"Jammy" (Lucky) = "Jeh-ah-meh-yeh"
K	"Keh"	"Kirk" (church) = "Kehrk"
L	"Leh"	"Lass" (girl) = "Lehss"
M	"Meh"	"Mingin'" (disgusting) = "Meng-in"
N	"Neh"	"Naw" (no) = "Neh"
O	"Oh"	"Bonnie" (beautiful) = "Boh-nee"

Letter	Pronunciation	Example
P	"Peh"	"Peely-wally" (pale) = "Peh-lee-wah-lee"
Q	"Kweh"	"Quine" (Girl) = "Kweh-eye-n"
R	"Rrrr" (rolled)	"Rabbit" = "Rrrr-abbit"
S	"Seh"	"Sassenach" (English person) = "Seh-seh-nahk"
T	"Teh"	"Tattie" (potato) = "Teh-tee"
U	"Ooh"	"Unco" (Strange) = "Ooh-neh-koh"
V	"Veh"	"Verra" (Very) = "Veh-rrrr-ah"
W	"Weh"	"Wee" (small) = "Weeh"
X	"Eks"	"X-ceptional" (Exceptional) = "Eks-sehp-teh-oh-nahl"
Y	"Yeh"	"Yer" (your) = "Yer"
Z	"Zeh"	"Zarrafact" (Is that a fact?) = "Zeh-ah-rrrr-ah-feh-ahk-teh"

2. Vowel Pronunciation

Vowel	Pronunciation	Example
A	"Ah"	"Braw" = "Brah"
E	"Eh"	"Ken" = "Kehn"
I	"Eye"	"Aye" = "Eye"
O	"Oh"	"Bonnie" = "Bon-ee"
U	"Ooh"	"Hoose" (house) = "Hooss"

3. Consonant Pronunciation

Consonant	Pronunciation	Example
R	Rolled or trilled	"Rabbit" = "Rrrr-abbit"
CH	Guttural "ch" (like "loch")	"Dreich" = "Dree-ch"
G	Hard "g" or silent	"Gie" = "Gee"

A TO Z
Essential Scottish Words and Expressions

Learn the most popular Scottish words and phrases to make you sound like a local. This chapter covers the essentials you'll hear and use in Scotland, from everyday greetings to playful slang.

A

Aboot

- Preposition: About.

- Example: "What are you talking aboot?"

- Cultural note: "Aboot" shows the characteristic vowel sounds in the Scottish accent. Scotland is very different when it comes to pronunciation. Knowing these differences will help you understand and communicate with Scottish speakers.

Auld

- Adjective: Old.

- Example: "He's an auld friend of mine."

- Cultural note: "Auld" is widely used in Scottish dialects and conveys a sense of respect for age and tradition. Using "auld" can add authenticity to your language and create a link to Scottish cultural heritage.

Awfy

- Adjective: Awful or very.

- Example: "It's awfy cold outside today."

- Cultural note: "Awfy" is often used to emphasize a statement. This is also a common feature of Scottish communication. it can help you express strong feelings or states.

Aye

- Adjective: Yes.

- Example: "Aye, I'll come along."

Cultural note: "Aye" is a basic word in the Scots language meaning "affirm or agree." Recognizing and using "Aye" can improve understanding and interaction with Scottish speakers.

Aye, right!

- Phrase: Used sarcastically to express disbelief or skepticism.

- Example: "You finished all your work? Aye, right!"

- Cultural note: "Aye, right!" Sometimes used playfully or sarcastically to express doubt or disbelief. This phrase will help you understand the subtleties of Scottish humor.

B

Bairn

- Noun: Child.

- Example: "The bairns are playing in the park."

- Cultural note: "Bairn" is a common term in both Scotland and the North of England, reflecting the importance of family and community in Scottish culture. It is used affectionately for children.

Baltic

- Adjective: Freezing.

- Example: "It's absolutely baltic outside today."

- Cultural note: "Baltic" is often used in Scotland to describe extremely cold weather. The term refers to the cold that prevails in the climate of the Baltic regions.

Bamp

- Noun: Grandfather (though more commonly used for a foolish person in Scottish slang).

- Example: "My bamp told me old stories."

- Cultural note: "Bamp" can mean both grandfather and foolish person, depending on the context. This illustrates the richness and versatility of Scottish slang.

Bampot

- Noun: Idiot or foolish person.

- Example: "Don't be a bampot!"

- Cultural note: "Bampot" is a light-hearted insult for someone who behaves foolishly. It is usually used playfully or teasingly by your friends.

Banging

- Adjective: Excellent, amazing.

- Example: "That gig was banging!"

- Cultural Note: "Banging" is a term used to describe something exceptionally good or exciting. It is often used when referring to music, parties, or events.

Banjaxed

- Adjective: Broken or ruined.

- Example: "My phone is banjaxed."

- Cultural note: "Banjaxed" is a descriptive term to describe something that is completely broken or beyond repair. In everyday life, we use it to complain when we buy things with damaged items.

Baw

- Noun: Ball.

- Example: "Pass me the baw."

- Cultural note: "Baw" is the Scottish word for ball and is often used in sports such as football. This shows how much the Scots love the game.

Bawheid/Bawheided

- Noun: Idiot or fool.

- Example: "Don't be such a bawheid."

- Cultural Note: "Bawheid" is another playful swear word to describe someone acting stupid. It's common to say it casually among friends.

Beaut

- Noun: A term of endearment for a female friend.

- Example: "She's an absolute beaut."

- Cultural note: "Beaut" is short for "beautiful" and is used affectionately to compliment a friend. It is a friendly expression that emphasizes affection and respect as well as a friendly relationship.

Belters

- Noun: Something excellent.

- Example: "That song is a belter!"

- Cultural note: "Belter" is used to describe something outstanding or fantastic, often in the context of music or a performance.

Ben

- Noun: Mountain.

- Example: "We climbed Ben Nevis."

- Cultural note: "Ben" is a Gaelic term for mountain, used mainly in Scotland. Many Scottish mountains have "Ben" in their name, for example, Ben Nevis, the highest mountain in the British Isles.

Bide

- Verb: Stay or wait.

- Example: "Bide here for a moment."

- Cultural note: "Bide" is an old Scottish word meaning "to linger" or "to wait". It is the time that people sometimes take for everything in Scotland, especially in the countryside.

Blag

- Verb: To bluff or deceive.

- Example: "He managed to blag his way into the club."

- Cultural note: "Blag" is used to successfully bluff or deceive someone. It is a term that means to be clever and cunning.

Blether

- Verb/Noun: To talk nonsense or chatter aimlessly.

- Example: "Stop blethering and get to the point."

- Cultural Note: "Blether" describes the spirit of friendly, aimless conversation. Everyone uses it to describe a casual and frivolous conversation between two people.

Blootered

- Adjective: Very drunk.

- Example: "He got blootered last night."

- Cultural Note: "Blootered" is a descriptive term for being very drunk. It is often used to describe a man who has eaten and drunk too much at a party.

Bonnie

- Adjective: Pretty or attractive.

- Example: "She's a bonnie lass."

- Cultural Note: "Bonnie" is commonly used to describe beauty and attractiveness. That is why it emphasizes the Scottish love for beauty and appeal.

Bottle

- Noun: Courage.

- Example: "He's got the bottle to do it."

- Cultural Note: "Bottle" is slang for courage or bravery. People use it to congratulate others for their skills and to confront challenges with assurance.

Braw

- Adjective: Great or good.

- Example: "That's a braw day out."

- Cultural Note: "Braw" is a versatile term used to describe something good or pleasing. It is a positive word and embraces the Scottish people's ethos of the need to do things right.

Breeks

- Noun: Trousers.

- Example: "Put on your best breeks for the party."

- Cultural Note: "Breeks" is a Scots term for trousers, often used in rural and traditional contexts. It focuses on how the Scots have a different word for almost everything in common use.

Bumfle

- Noun: Mess or untidy bundle.

- Example: "Your room is a right bumfle."

- Cultural Note: "Bumfle" is used to describe a disorganized or untidy situation. It is a term that refers to the state of organization and sanitation.

Burn

- Noun: Stream or small river.

- Example: "We followed the burn down the valley."

- Cultural Note: "Burn" is a common term in Scotland for a small stream or river. It is very popular in toponyms and describes the nature of the country's terrain.

Butty

- Noun: Friend or mate.

- Example: "How's it going, butty?"

- Cultural Note: "Butty" is a term of friendship and camaraderie. It is known to be used casually to refer to a friend or a companion

C

Cannae

- Verb: Cannot.

- Example: "I cannae believe it!"

- Cultural Note: "Cannae" is a familiar contraction in Scottish dialect as a result of the pronunciation and style of Scots. It is usually employed to signify the impossibility of something as far as is concerned.

Canny

- Adjective: Careful, clever, or cautious.

- Example: "He's a canny lad."

- Cultural Note: The Scots have a very special value for intelligence and frugality, and that is why the word "Canny" is so universal. It can be applied to a person that is cautious and wise.

Ceilidh

- Noun: A social gathering with music and dancing.

- Example: "We're going to a ceilidh tonight."

- Cultural Note: A "Ceilidh" is a Scottish social occasion where dance, story-telling, music, and other forms of entertainment are used culturally. It is very much a Scottish tradition and is performed during any occasion or festival.

Chancer

- Noun: Someone who takes risks or chances.

- Example: "He's a bit of a chancer."

- Cultural Note: "Chancer" refers to someone who tends to take risks, big risks but in a risky manner, in this case, the risky manner is opportunistic. It also reflects the Scots' understanding of risk-taking and daring.

Chookie

- Noun: Chicken or bird.

- Example: "The chookies are in the yard."

- Cultural Note: "Chookie" is an affectionate term for a chicken or small bird, often used in rural areas. It highlights the Scots' connection to farm life and nature.

Clarty

- Adjective: Dirty or muddy.

- Example: "Your boots are clarty!"

- Cultural Note: "Clarty" is used to describe something dirty or muddy. It's a practical term often used in the context of Scotland's wet and muddy climate.

Clipe

- Verb: To tell tales or inform someone.

- Example: "Don't Clipe on me!"

- Cultural Note: "Clipe" is used to describe someone who tells tales or informs on others. Usually, it has rather negative meanings associated with it, referring to betrayal or lack of trust.

Cludgie

- Noun: Toilet.

- Example: "Where's the cludgie?"

- Cultural Note: "Cludgie" is a colloquial term for the toilet. Sometimes people prefer using this term probably due to its informal nature because it's a light word that may be used often in day-to-day conversation.

Coo

- Noun: Cow.

- Example: "The coos are in the field."

- Cultural Note: "Coo" is the Scots term for cow, reflecting the traditional farming culture of Scotland. It is evident in the rural and agricultural areas.

Coorie

- Verb: Snuggle or cuddle.

- Example: "Let's coorie in by the fire."

- Cultural Note: "Coorie" is a term that conveys a sense of warmth and comfort. It's often associated with the Scottish lifestyle of seeking coziness in a rugged climate.

Crabit

- Adjective: Irritable.

- Example: "He's always crabbit in the morning."

- Cultural Note: "Crabit" is a vivid descriptor of mood, commonly used to describe someone irritable or grumpy. That is because the selection captures the emotive character of Scottish vernacular language.

Craic

- Noun: Fun or entertainment.

- Example: "We had a great craic last night."

- Cultural Note: "Craic" (also spelled "crack") is an Irish term that has been adopted into Scottish slang. It represents good times, lively conversation, and entertainment, often in a social setting.

Cudie

- Noun: Horse or donkey.

- Example: "The cuddie is in the stable."

- Cultural Note: "Cuddie" is a term used for a horse or donkey, reflecting Scotland's agricultural heritage. It's often used in rural contexts and highlights the importance of these animals in farm life.

D

Dae

- Verb: Do.

- Example: "What did ye dae that for?"

- Cultural Note: "Dae" is a common Scots word reflecting the distinct pronunciation and dialect of the region. It is a prerequisite term used to explain and express the Scots language.

Daft

- Adjective: Stupid or silly.

- Example: "Don't be daft!"

- Cultural Note: "Daft" is widely used to describe foolish or silly behavior. It is a casual term that is generally not taken seriously most of the time it is used.

Daftie

- Noun: Silly person.

- Example: "He's a right daftie."

- Cultural Note: "Daftie" is an affectionate term for someone who is acting foolishly. It is mostly said in-jokes between friends.

Dander

- Noun/Verb: Walk or stroll.

- Example: "Let's go for a dander."

- Cultural Note: "Dander" is a term used to describe a leisurely walk. It also focuses on taking time just to sit, breathe, and enjoy the environment.

Dee Ye Ken?

- Phrase: Do You Understand?

- Example: "Dee ye ken what I'm saying?"

- Cultural Note: "Dee Ye Ken?" It is a common question in Scots, to check for an understanding.

Dinger

- Noun: A hard hit or punch.

- Example: "He gave him a right dinger."

- Cultural Note: "Dinger" is a term used to describe a strong physical impact. In sports or physical confrontations, it's often used.

Dinnae

- Verb: Don't.

- Example: "Dinnae forget your keys."

- Cultural Note: "Dinnae" is a contraction commonly used in Scots to mean "don't."

Dobber

- Noun: A fool.

- Example: "He's a total dobber."

- Cultural Note: "Dobber" is a light insult used to describe someone acting foolishly. But it's often used in a teasing, nonserious way between friends.

Dochanadors

- Noun: Hands.

- Example: "Keep yer dochanadors to yersel'."

- Cultural Note: "Dochanadors" is a less common term for hands, reflecting the rich and varied vocabulary of Scots. It's often used humorously.

Dodgy

- Adjective: Suspicious, unreliable.

- Example: "That deal sounds dodgy."

- Cultural Note: "Dodgy" is used to describe something or someone that appears untrustworthy. It's a practical term for what can be identified as potential risks.

Dook

- Verb/Noun: Dip or bathe.

- Example: "We had a dook in the loch."

- Cultural Note: "Dook" is a term used to describe taking a dip or swim, often in natural water bodies like lochs or rivers. It shows Scotland's relationship with its natural landscape.

Doric

- Noun: The dialect of Scots spoken in the Northeast of Scotland.

- Example: "He speaks fluent Doric."

- Cultural Note: "Doric" is a distinctive dialect of Scots, with its unique vocabulary and pronunciation. It's mainly spoken in Aberdeenshire and surrounding areas.

Doss

- Verb/Noun: Sleep or a place to sleep.

- Example: "I need a place to doss tonight."

- Cultural Note: "Doss" is used to describe sleeping or a place to sleep, often informally. It's a term that means rest and shelter.

Dour

- Adjective: Grim or sullen.

- Example: "He's got a dour expression."

- Cultural Note: "Dour" is used to describe someone serious, grim, or sullen. It reflects the Scots' ability to convey deep emotions with simple words.

Dreich

- Adjective: Dull, dreary, or miserable, often used to describe the weather.

- Example: "It's a dreich day outside."

- Cultural Note: "Dreich" perfectly encapsulates Scotland's often rainy and overcast weather. It's a descriptive term that helps to describe the effect of the climate on Scottish life.

Drookit

- Adjective: Very wet or soaked.

- Example: "I got drookit in the rain."

- Cultural Note: "Drookit" is used to describe being completely soaked, often due to Scotland's frequent rain. It's a vivid term for the amount of wetness.

Dunderheid

- Noun: Stupid.

- Example: "Don't be such a dunderheid."

- Cultural Note: "Dunderheid" is a playful term for someone who is acting foolishly or stupidly. While it's often used humorously by friends and family.

E

Eejit

- Noun: Idiot.

- Example: "Don't be such an eejit!"

- Cultural Note: "Eejit" is a playful and affectionate term for calling someone an idiot. It is most commonly used informally amongst friends and family and so is considered more of Scottish slang.

Eh?

- Phrase: What did you say?

- Example: "Eh? Could you repeat that?"

- Cultural Note: "Eh?" is the phrase that Scots use when somebody has spoken and they did not quite catch the last part of what was said. It is an easy, colloquial means of asking for a repetition of a conversation in the course of a conversation.

Eldritch

- Adjective: Weird or eerie.

- Example: "There was an eldritch glow in the forest."

- Cultural Note: "Eldritch" is a term used to describe something strange or supernatural. It reflects Scotland's rich folklore and storytelling traditions, often associated with the mystical and eerie.

Ersed

- Adjective: Can't Be Bothered.-

- Example: "I'm too ersed to go out tonight."

- Cultural Note: "Ersed" is a colloquial way of expressing a lack of motivation or interest in doing something. Its most common use is to give the impression of idleness or reluctance.

F

Fae

- Preposition: From.

- Example: "She's fae Glasgow."

- Cultural Note: "Fae" is a common Scots preposition meaning "from." It reflects the distinct vocabulary and pronunciation of Scottish dialects, adding authenticity to conversations.

Faff

- Verb: To waste time.

- Example: "Stop faffing around and get to work."

- Cultural Note: "Faff" is used to describe unnecessary or time-wasting activities. It's a practical term often used to encourage efficiency and focus.

Fankle

- Noun: A mess or tangle.

- Example: "The cables are in a fankle."

- Cultural Note: "Fankle" is a descriptive term for a tangled or messy situation.

Fash

- Verb: To bother or annoy.

- Example: "Don't fash yersel' about it."

- Cultural Note: "Fash" is a term used to describe causing trouble or annoyance. It's often used to calm someone down, indicating that they shouldn't worry.

Feart

- Adjective: Afraid.

- Example: "I'm no feart of anything."

- Cultural Note: "Feart" is a commonly used term to express fear or apprehension.

Feg

- Noun: Cigarette.

- Example: "Can I borrow a feg?"

- Cultural Note: "Feg" is an informal term for a cigarette.

Fifer

- Noun: Person from Fife.

- Example: "She's a true Fifer."

- Cultural Note: "Fifer" is used to describe someone from the Fife region in Scotland. It draws attention to the region and its people.

Fit

- Pronoun: What.

- Example: "Fit are you talking about?"

- Cultural Note: "Fit" is the Scots term for "what," reflecting the distinctive vocabulary and pronunciation of Scottish dialects. It is usually found in casual conversation.

Fitba/Footie

- Noun: Football (soccer).

- Example: "Are you going to the fitba match?"

- Cultural Note: "Fitba" is the Scots term for football (soccer).

Fleg

- Verb: To frighten or scare.

- Example: "He flegged me with that story."

- Cultural Note: "Fleg" is used to describe causing fear or alarm. It is a working term used in narrations or to express responses.

Fly

- Adjective: Clever or sneaky.

- Example: "That was a fly move."

- Cultural Note: "Fly" describes someone clever or cunning, often in a sneaky way.

Foos yer doos

- Phrase: How are you?

- Example: "Foos yer doos today?"

- Cultural Note: "Foos yer doos" is a friendly greeting in Scots, equivalent to asking "How are you?".

Fooshtie

- Adjective: Weak or feeble.

- Example: "He's feeling a bit fooshtie."

- Cultural Note: "Fooshtie" is used to describe someone who is weak or not feeling well. It is a word which is used under circumstances of expressing care for a person's wellbeing.

G

Gadgie

- Noun: Old man.

- Example: "That auld gadgie lives down the lane."

- Cultural Note: "Gadgie" is an affectionate or sometimes humorous term for an old man. It speaks to the Scots' knack for producing cute and unusual words for people in their community.

Gads

- Exclamation: Exclamation of disgust.

- Example: "Gads, that's disgusting!"

- Cultural Note: "Gads" is a strong expression of disgust or distaste. This is a powerful word used to describe an immediate reaction to something that isn't so pleasant.

Gallus

- Adjective: Bold, daring, or confident.

- Example: "She walked in with a gallus attitude."

- Cultural Note: "Gallus" describes someone who is confident and daring. Often used to praise someone's boldness and audacity.

Galoot

- Noun: Clumsy.

- Example: "You're such a galoot, always tripping over things."

- Cultural Note: "Galoot" is a light-hearted term for a clumsy person. Especially when used humorously, it's sometimes used to describe someone's awkward movements.

Gammie

- Noun: Game or sport.

- Example: "Let's have a gammie of cards."

- Cultural Note: "Gammie" refers to any game or sport. It says something about the Scots' love of recreational activities and friendly competition.

Gammy

- Adjective: Something wrong or not working properly.

- Example: "I've got a gammy leg today."

- Cultural Note: "Gammy" is used to describe something that is not functioning correctly. Physical ailments and malfunctioning objects are the usual application.

Gansey

- Noun: Sweater or jumper.

- Example: "I need my gansey for this cold weather."

- Cultural Note: "Gansey" is a traditional term for a knitted sweater, often worn by fishermen.

Gaunnie

- Phrase: Going to.

- Example: "I'm gaunnie head out soon."

- Cultural Note: "Gaunnie" is a colloquial way of saying "going to."

Gawk

- Verb: Stare or gape.

- Example: "Stop gawking at me."

- Cultural Note: "Gawk" is used to describe staring or looking at something with wide eyes. Often it means that staring is rude or inappropriate.

Geegie

- Noun: Mouth.

- Example: "Shut your geegie and listen."

- Cultural Note: "Geegie" is a playful term for mouth. This is the Scots' ability to invent hilarious words for everyday body parts.

Gie it laldy!

- Phrase: Give it your best shot.

- Example: "When you perform, gie it laldy!"

- Cultural Note: "Gie it laldy" encourages full effort and enthusiasm.

Gie us a bell!

- Phrase: Give me a call.

- Example: "Gie us a bell when you're free."

- Cultural Note: "Gie us a bell" is a friendly way of asking someone to call you. It shows that the connection and social relationships are important.

Gie

- Verb: Give.

- Example: "Gie me a hand with this."

- Cultural Note: "Gie" is the Scots word for "give," showcasing the distinct vocabulary and pronunciation of the dialect.

Ginger

- Noun: Another word for fizzy juice.

- Example: "I'll have a bottle of ginger, please."

- Cultural Note: "Ginger" is commonly used in Scotland to refer to fizzy drinks or soda. It's a local colloquial term.

Glaickit

- Adjective: Not very clever.

- Example: "He's a bit glaickit."

- Cultural Note: "Glaickit" is a term used to describe someone who isn't very sharp or clever. It's mostly used in a joking or humorous setting.

Glaur

- Noun: Mud or muck.

- Example: "The fields are full of glaur after the rain."

- Cultural Note: "Glaur" is used to describe muddy or mucky conditions, reflecting Scotland's wet climate and the common presence of mud in rural areas.

Gob

- Noun: Mouth.

- Example: "Shut your gob."

- Cultural Note: "Gob" is a slang term for mouth, often used humorously or bluntly. It's a way to tell someone to stop talking.

Gobsmacked

- Adjective: Astonished, amazed.

- Example: "I was gobsmacked by the news."

- Cultural Note: "Gobsmacked" is a vivid term for being utterly astonished or amazed. It's a strong expression of surprise and is used in response to unexpected events.

Gonny

- Phrase: Going to.

- Example: "I'm gonny head out soon."

- Cultural Note: "Gonny" is a contraction used in Scots to mean "going to." Often, this is used in everyday speech about convenience and ease.

Gowk

- Noun: Fool or idiot.

- Example: "Don't be such a gowk."

- Cultural Note: "Gowk" is a term used to describe someone acting foolishly. Friends and family often use it humorously.

Grand

- Adjective: Excellent, fine.

- Example: "Everything is grand."

- Cultural Note: "Grand" is used to describe something excellent or satisfactory. It's a good term that people use to convey approval or contentment.

Greet

- Verb: To cry or weep.

- Example: "The bairn is greeting again."

- Cultural Note: "Greet" is the Scots term for crying or weeping. It's the simplest expression of emotion.

Gub

- Noun: Mouth.

- Example: "Shut yer gub."

- Cultural Note: "Gub" is a Scots term for mouth, similar to "gob." It's usually employed humorously or bluntly to tell someone to shut up.

Gubbed

- Adjective: Exhausted or beaten.

- Example: "I'm totally gubbed after that run."

- Cultural Note: "Gubbed" describes being completely exhausted or defeated. Often used to describe physical or emotional fatigue, it's a vivid term.

Guff

- Noun: Nonsense or bad smell.

- Example: "Stop talking guff."

- Cultural Note: "Guff" is used to describe nonsensical talk or an unpleasant smell. But it's a flexible term and can apply to both speech and sensory experiences.

H

Hackit

- Adjective: Ugly.

- Example: "That painting is hackit."

- Cultural Note: "Hackit" is a term for something unattractive. It is one of the simplest words commonly used to convey disapproval of something's appearance.

Haver

- Verb: To talk nonsense.

- Example: "Stop haverin' and tell me the truth."

- Cultural Note: "Haver" is used to describe speaking nonsense or talking aimlessly. It is an operational term for referring to meaningless talk.

Heid

- Noun: Head.

- Example: "I bumped my heid."

- Cultural Note: "Heid" is the Scots term for head.

Hing

- Verb: Hang.

- Example: "Hing your coat up, please."

- Cultural Note: "Hing" is the Scots word for hang.

Hoachin

- Adjective: Very busy or crowded.

- Example: "The market was hoachin today."

- Cultural Note: "Hoachin" is used to describe a place that is very busy or crowded. They suggest a feeling of activity, which in most cases is associated with crowded territories.

Hogmanay

- Noun: New Year's Eve.

- Example: "We're celebrating Hogmanay with fireworks."

- Cultural Note: "Hogmanay" is the Scots word for New Year's Eve, a significant celebration in Scotland marked by festivities and traditions.

Honkin

- Adjective: Very large.

- Example: "That's a honkin piece of cake!"

- Cultural Note: "Honkin" is used to describe something very large in size. In this case, it is employed in order to stress how massive an object is.

Hoose

- Noun: House.

- Example: "We're going back to the hoose."

- Cultural Note: "Hoose" is the Scots term for house.

Houghin

- Adjective: Disgusting.

- Example: "That smell is houghin."

- Cultural Note: "Houghin" is a strong term used to describe something disgusting or unpleasant. It is often used to say how much you detest something.

How

- Adjective: Why.

- Example: "How did you do that?"

- Cultural Note: "How" is used in Scots to mean "why," showcasing the distinct vocabulary and usage of the dialect. This is an important word to know and to use in speaking Scots.

Howfin

- Adjective: Smelly or foul.

- Example: "That bin is howfin!"

- Cultural Note: "Howfin" is used to describe something that has a bad smell. The term is often used to describe how people respond to unpleasant odors, in a vivid way.

Hunners

- Noun: Hundreds.

- Example: "There were hunners of people at the concert."

- Cultural Note: "Hunners" is a colloquial term for hundreds, often used to emphasize large numbers.

I

Innit

- Phrase: Isn't it?

- Example: "It's a great day, innit?"

- Cultural Note: "Innit" is a colloquial contraction of "isn't it?" It's often used to emphasize something or to get agreement in a conversation.

Isnae

- Phrase: Is not.

- Example: "That isnae my fault."

- Cultural Note: "Isnae" is a Scots contraction for "is not." It features dialect vocabulary and pronunciation with a more conversational sound to the speech.

J

Jammy

- Adjective: Lucky.

- Example: "You're so jammy, winning that prize!"

- Cultural Note: "Jammy" is a playful term used to describe someone who is fortunate. It is usually used to show a surprise bit of good luck.

Jeely piece

- Noun: A jam sandwich.

- Example: "I packed a jeely piece for lunch."

- Cultural Note: "Jeely piece" is a Scots term for a jam sandwich. It's a simple and traditional snack, often associated with childhood and nostalgia.

Jings!

- Exclamation: An expression of surprise.

- Example: "Jings! I didn't see that coming!"

- Cultural Note: "Jings!" is an exclamation for surprise or astonishment. It's a mild way to say that you are shocked.

K

Keek

- Verb: Peek or glance.

- Example: "Have a keek out the window."

- Cultural Note: "Keek" is a Scots term for a quick look or glance. It's often used in a playful context, reflecting the Scots' ability to create engaging and vivid language.

Ken

- Verb: Know or understand.

- Example: "Do ye ken what I mean?"

- Cultural Note: "Ken" is an essential Scots term meaning "know" or "understand." It's widely used in everyday conversation and is a key part of the dialect.

Kerry Oot

- Noun: Takeaway food.

- Example: "Let's get a kerry oot for dinner."

- Cultural Note: "Kerry oot" is the Scots term for takeaway food, reflecting the local pronunciation. It's commonly used when referring to meals bought from restaurants to be eaten elsewhere.

Kip

- Noun/Verb: Sleep or nap.

- Example: "I need a kip before we go out."

- Cultural Note: "Kip" is a term used to describe sleep or a nap. It's a common and practical term in Scots, reflecting the importance of rest.

L

Laddie

- Noun: Young man or boy.

- Example: "That laddie has a lot of energy."

- Cultural Note: "Laddie" is an affectionate term for a young man or boy. It is a Scots way of calling younger males with a warm and friendly tone.

Laldie

- Phrase: To do something with great energy.

- Example: "He gave it laldie at the concert."

- Cultural Note: "Laldie" is used to describe putting great effort and enthusiasm into an activity. It is the Scots-spirited approach to life.

Lassie

- Noun: Young woman or girl.

- Example: "That lassie is very kind."

- Cultural Note: "Lassie" is an affectionate term for a young woman or girl. It's used widely in Scotland to address females in a friendly, familiar manner.

Loan

- Noun: Lane.

- Example: "They live down a quiet loan."

- Cultural Note: "Loan" is the Scots word for lane, reflecting the rural and quaint aspects of Scottish life. Narrow country roads are often used to describe it.

Lug

- Noun: Ear.

- Example: "He whispered in my lug."

- Cultural Note: "Lug" is the Scots term for ear.

Lush

- Adjective: Lovely, great.

- Example: "That garden looks lush."

- Cultural Note: "Lush" is used to describe something lovely or excellent. It often means that it is abundant and attractive growth, and is admiring of beauty and quality.

M

Mad wi it

- Phrase: Very enthusiastic or excited.

- Example: "He was mad wi it at the party."

- Cultural Note: "Mad wi it" is used to describe someone extremely enthusiastic or excited. This is one of those high-energy, spirited nature that is often seen in Scottish celebrations.

Manky

- Adjective: Dirty or unpleasant.

- Example: "Your shoes are manky."

- Cultural Note: "Manky" is a term used to describe something dirty or unpleasant. A practical word often used to express distaste for uncleanliness.

Maw

- Noun: Mother.

- Example: "My maw makes the best haggis."

- Cultural Note: "Maw" is a colloquial term for mother, reflecting the informal and affectionate language used in Scots families.

Messages

- Noun: Groceries.

- Example: "I'm off to get the messages."

- Cultural Note: "Messages" is the Scots term for groceries or shopping.

Mince

- Noun: Nonsense.

- Example: "That story is pure mince."

- Cultural Note: "Mince" is used to describe something as nonsense or rubbish. It is often used to label false or exaggerated claims.

Mind

- Verb: Remember.

- Example: "Mind to lock the door."

- Cultural Note: "Mind" is commonly used in Scots to mean "remember." The term is practical and is used in reminders or instructions.

Mingin

- Adjective: Revolting.

- Example: "That food is mingin."

- Cultural Note: "Mingin" is a strong term used to describe something revolting or disgusting. It's often used to describe strong negative reactions to taste, smell, or appearance.

Mither

- Noun: Mother.

- Example: "My mither called me today."

- Cultural Note: "Mither" is another Scots term for mother, reflecting the rich variety of words used to describe family members in Scottish dialects.

Mony

- Adjective: Many.

- Example: "There are mony reasons to visit Scotland."

- Cultural Note: "Mony" is Scot's word for "many".

Muckle

- Adjective: Large or a lot.

- Example: "That's a muckle fish you've caught!"

- Cultural Note: "Muckle" is an expressive term used to describe something large or in great quantity.

N

Nae/Naw

- Phrase: No.

- Example: "Nae, I don't need any help."

- Cultural Note: "Nae" or "Naw" are Scots terms for "no." These are very important parts of the dialect and are used every day.

Nappeer

- Noun: Head.

- Example: "I bumped my nappeer."

- Cultural Note: "Nappeer" is the Scots term for head.

Ned

- Noun: Hooligan or Troublemaker.

- Example: "That group of neds is causing trouble."

- Cultural Note: "Ned" is a term used to describe a young troublemaker or hooligan. It has negative meanings, which are also related to the youth behavior problems existing in this society.

Neep

- Noun: Turnip.

- Example: "We're having neeps and tatties for dinner."

- Cultural Note: "Neep" is the Scots word for turnip, often used in traditional dishes like "neeps and tatties," a staple in Scottish cuisine.

Noo

- Adjective: Now.

- Example: "We're leaving right noo."

- Cultural Note: "Noo" is the Scots word for "now"

Numpty

- Noun: A stupid person.

- Example: "Don't be such a numpty."

- Cultural Note: "Numpty" is a popular joke among friends and family to someone who behaves foolishly.

O

Och

- Exclamation: Expression of surprise or frustration.

- Example: "Och, I forgot my keys!"

- Cultural Note: "Och" is a versatile exclamation used to express surprise, frustration, or resignation.

Oot

- Adjective: Out.

- Example: "I'm going oot for a walk."

- Cultural Note: "Oot" is the Scots term for "out"

Outwith

- Preposition: Outside of or beyond.

- Example: "This issue is outwith my control."

- Cultural Note: "Outwith" is a formal Scots term meaning "outside of" or "beyond."

Oxter

- Noun: Armpit.

- Example: "He tickled my oxter."

- Cultural Note: "Oxter" is the Scots term for armpit.

P

Patter

- Noun: Banter or chat.

- Example: "He's got great patter."

- Cultural Note: "Patter" refers to light-hearted banter or conversation, often humorous and engaging.

Peely-wally

- Adjective: Pale or unwell.

- Example: "You're looking a bit peely-wally today."

- Cultural Note: "Peely-wally" is used to describe someone who looks pale or unwell. It's a word that people use to say that someone is not okay.

Piece

- Noun: Sandwich.

- Example: "I packed a piece for lunch."

- Cultural Note: "Piece" is the Scots term for a sandwich, commonly used in everyday conversation.

Plook

- Noun: Pimple.

- Example: "I've got a big plook on my chin."

- Cultural Note: "Plook" is a term used to describe a pimple, reflecting the Scots' ability to create unique and descriptive words for everyday occurrences.

Poke

- Noun: Ice cream cone or bag.

- Example: "I'll have a poke of chips, please."

- Cultural Note: "Poke" is a versatile term used to describe an ice cream cone or a small bag, especially for food items.

Polis

- Noun: Police.

- Example: "The polis are patrolling the area."

- Cultural Note: "Polis" is the Scots term for police, showcasing the distinct vocabulary and pronunciation of the dialect.

Puggled

- Adjective: Tired out.

- Example: "I'm feeling puggled after that workout."

- Cultural Note: "Puggled" is used to describe being very tired or exhausted. It's a vivid term that conveys a strong sense of fatigue.

Pure mince

- Phrase: Bewildered.

- Example: "That explanation was pure mince."

- Cultural Note: "Pure mince" is used to describe something completely nonsensical or confusing. And it's often used to criticize vague or convoluted statements.

Pure

- Adjective: Very or really (e.g., "pure dead brilliant" means "very good").

- Example: "She's pure kind-hearted."

- Cultural Note: "Pure" is used in Scots to intensify adjectives, meaning very or really. It's a word that can be used to add emphasis to descriptions.

Puss

- Noun: Face.

- Example: "Wipe that frown off your puss."

- Cultural Note: "Puss" is the Scots term for face, often used playfully or humorously.

Q

Quine

- Noun: Girl.

- Example: "That quine is very talented."

- Cultural Note: "Quine" is a term used in the Doric dialect of Scots, primarily spoken in the northeast of Scotland. It's commonly used to refer to a girl or young woman and highlights the regional variations within Scottish slang.

R

Radge

- Adjective: Crazy or wild.

- Example: "He went radge at the party."

- Cultural Note: "Radge" is used to describe someone who is acting crazy or wild.

Reek

- Verb/Noun: Smoke or smell strongly.

- Example: "The kitchen reeked of burnt toast."

- Cultural Note: "Reek" is used to describe a strong smell, often unpleasant, or the presence of smoke. It's a practical word that can be used in many situations.

Riddy

- Adjective: Embarrassed (red-faced).

- Example: "I was pure riddy after that mistake."

- Cultural Note: "Riddy" is used to describe someone embarrassed and red-faced. A playful and descriptive term for the physical reaction to embarrassment.

S

Sassenach

- Noun: English person.

- Example: "He's a Sassenach, but he loves Scotland."

- Cultural Note: "Sassenach" is a term used by Scots to refer to English people. It may be used either neutrally or affectionately with either Scotland and England being historically and culturally 'neighbours' being close.

Scooby

- Noun: Clue.

- Example: "I haven't a scooby what's going on."

- Cultural Note: "Scooby" is derived from the phrase "Scooby-Doo" and is used to mean a clue. It's frequently used in a light hearted, humorous way.

Scran

- Noun: Food.

- Example: "Let's get some scran, I'm starving."

- Cultural Note: "Scran" is a Scots term for food, commonly used in meals conversation.

Scrieve

- Verb: To write.

- Example: "I need to scrieve a letter to my friend."

- Cultural Note: "Scrieve" is the Scots term for writing. It's used in both formal and informal context.

Scunnered

- Adjective: Fed up or bored.

- Example: "I'm scunnered with all this rain."

- Cultural Note: "Scunnered" conveys a strong feeling of frustration or annoyance. It's used to describe a feeling of general tiredness or frustration.

Shan

- Adjective: A shame or a pity.

- Example: "It's a shan you missed the party."

- Cultural Note: "Shan" is used to express that something is a shame or pity.

Shooftie

- Noun: A glance or look.

- Example: "Give it a quick shooftie and see if it's okay."

- Cultural Note: "Shooftie" is a term used for taking a quick glance or look. It's often used in casual conversation.

Shoogle

- Verb: To shake or wobble.

- Example: "The table was shoogling."

- Cultural Note: "Shoogle" is used to describe something that is shaking or wobbling.

Shouther

- Noun: Shoulder.

- Example: "He patted me on the shouther."

- Cultural Note: "Shouther" is the Scots term for shoulder.

Skelf

- Noun: Splinter.

- Example: "I've got a skelf in my finger."

- Cultural Note: "Skelf" is used to describe a small splinter of wood.

Skelp

- Verb/Noun: Slap.

- Example: "He gave him a skelp on the back."

- Cultural Note: "Skelp" is used to describe a slap or light hit. It's also used playfully or to refer to a minor physical reprimand.

Skive

- Verb: To avoid work or responsibility.

- Example: "He's always skiving off work."

- Cultural Note: "Skive" is used to describe avoiding work or responsibilities. It is a practical term used to describe behaviour at school or work.

Slecher

- Adjective: Messy or clumsy.

- Example: "Your room is so slecher."

- Cultural Note: "Slecher" is used to describe someone who is messy or clumsy. It is usually used humorously to describe untidy, or awkward behavior.

Sleekit

- Adjective: Sly or cunning.

- Example: "He's a sleekit one, always scheming."

- Cultural Note: "Sleekit" describes someone who is sly or cunning.

Smirr

- Noun: Light rain.

- Example: "It's just a smirr, no need for an umbrella."

- Cultural Note: "Smirr" is used to describe a light drizzle or misty rain. A common weather term in Scotland and referring to the frequent light rain in the Scottish climate.

Snash

- Noun: Verbal abuse.

- Example: "He gave me a load of snash."

- Cultural Note: "Snash" is used to describe verbal abuse or harsh words. Strong term used to express displeasure with someone's speech.

Snell

- Adjective: Sharp.

- Example: "The wind is snell today."

- Cultural Note: "Snell" is used to describe something sharp, often referring to the weather. it's the word for the intensity of cold winds or sharp conditions.

Snib

- Noun/Verb: Lock or latch.

- Example: "Make sure to snib the door."

- Cultural Note: "Snib" is used to describe a lock or latch, or the action of locking. This is a practical term you often see in household contexts.

Sook

- Verb/Noun: Sulk or suck up.

- Example: "Stop being a sook."

- Cultural Note: "Sook" is used to describe someone who is sulking or trying to gain favor through flattery. It's a straightforward term often used to describe behavior.

Sorted

- Adjective/Verb: Okay, understood, agreed.

- Example: "Everything's sorted now."

- Cultural Note: "Sorted" is used to confirm that something is okay, understood, or agreed upon. A practical term meaning resolution or agreement.

Sporran

- Noun: Pouch worn with a kilt.

- Example: "He kept his money in his sporran."

- Cultural Note: "Sporran" is a traditional Scottish pouch worn with a kilt. It is Scottish cultural heritage and traditional dress.

Stoatin

- Adjective: Excellent or fantastic.

- Example: "That gig was stoatin!"

- Cultural Note: "Stoatin" is used to describe something that is excellent or fantastic. This a very positive term used to express a feeling.

Stookie

- Noun: Plaster cast.

- Example: "He's got a stookie on his arm."

- Cultural Note: "Stookie" is the Scots term for a plaster cast used to set broken bones. This is a simple term for practical medical treatment.

Stoor

- Noun: Dust.

- Example: "The attic is full of stoor."

- Cultural Note: "Stoor" is used to describe dust or fine particles. You hear this term thrown around all the time in household contexts.

Stramash

- Noun: Commotion or uproar.

- Example: "There was a stramash at the pub."

- Cultural Note: "Stramash" is used to describe a commotion or uproar.

Stum

- Verb: To stumble or trip.

- Example: "I stummed over the rock."

- Cultural Note: "Stum" is used to describe stumbling or tripping.

Swa

- Adverb: So.

- Example: "It was swa cold outside."

- Cultural Note: "Swa" is the Scots term for "so," reflecting the distinct vocabulary and pronunciation of the dialect.

T

Tattie

- Noun: Potato.

- Example: "We're having mince and tatties for dinner."

Cultural Insight: The word "Tattie" refers to potatoes in the Scottish dialect, underscoring their significance in Scottish cuisine. Potatoes are key ingredients in classic dishes such as "tatties and neeps."

Telt

- Verb: Told.

- Example: "I telt you to be careful."

- Cultural Note: "Telt" is Scot's word for "told,".

Thon

- Pronoun: That.

- Example: "Pass me thon book."

- Cultural Note: "Thon" is the Scots term for "that," reflecting the unique vocabulary of the dialect.

Tidy

- Adjective: Neat or well-organized.

- Example: "Your room looks tidy."

- Cultural Note: "Tidy" is used to describe something neat and well-organized. It is a simple term used to compliment cleanliness and orderliness.

Tod

- Noun: Fox.

- Example: "There's a tod in the garden."

Cultural Insight: "Tod" is the Scots word for a fox.

Tumshie

- Noun: Turnip.

- Example: "We're having tumshie soup tonight."

- Cultural Note: "Tumshie" is another Scots term for turnip, similar to "neep." Traditional dishes use it often, and it represents Scotland's agricultural heritage.

U

Unco

- Adjective: Strange or unusual.

- Example: "That's an unco story."

- Cultural Note: "Unco" is used to describe something strange or unusual. It reflects the Scots' ability to capture the essence of the unfamiliar or peculiar with a single word.

V

Vennel

- Noun: Alleyway.

- Example: "They walked through the narrow vennel."

- Cultural Note: "Vennel" is used to describe a narrow alleyway or lane, commonly found in Scottish towns and cities. It reflects the historic and compact urban planning typical of older Scottish settlements.

Verra

- Adjective: Very.

- Example: "That's a verra nice gesture."

- Cultural Note: "Verra" is the Scots term for "very," showcasing the special pronunciation of the dialect.

W

Wabbit

- Adjective: Tired or worn out.

- Example: "I'm feeling wabbit after that long walk."

- Cultural Note: "Wabbit" is used to describe someone exhausted. It's a usual term often used to express fatigue.

Wame

- Noun: Stomach.

- Example: "My wame is full after that meal."

- Cultural Note: "Wame" is the Scots term for stomach.

Wan

- Adjective/Noun: One.

- Example: "Just give me the wan book."

- Cultural Note: "Wan" is the Scots term for "one".

Wean

- Noun: Small child.

- Example: "The weans are playing outside."

- Cultural Note: "Wean" is a term used to refer to a small child, derived from the phrase "wee ane" (little one)

Wee

- Adjective: Small or little.

- Example: "That's a wee kitten."

- Cultural Note: "Wee" is perhaps one of the most recognizable Scottish terms, used affectionately to describe something small or cute. It's a common term of endearment used in Scotland.

Wheesht

- Verb/Noun: Quiet.

- Example: "Wheesht, we're trying to watch the film."

- Cultural Note: "Wheesht" is used to tell someone to be quiet. It's usually used with a humorous or gentle tone to quiet someone.

Whit

- Pronoun: What.

- Example: "Whit are you talking about?"

- Cultural Note: "Whit" is the Scots term for "what," reflecting the distinct vocabulary and pronunciation of Scottish dialects.

Wicked

- Adjective: Excellent, amazing.

- Example: "That performance was wicked!"

- Cultural Note: "Wicked" is used to describe something excellent.

Windae

- Noun: Window.

- Example: "Close the windae, it's cold outside."

- Cultural Note: "Windae" is Scot's term for "Window".

Wingnut

- Noun: Someone with big ears.

- Example: "He's called a wingnut because of his ears."

- Cultural Note: "Wingnut" is a humorous term used to describe someone with big ears. The Scottish slang is always playful and descriptive, and this reflects that.

Wummin

- Noun: Woman.

- Example: "That wummin is very kind."

- Cultural Note: "Wummin" is the Scots term for woman.

X

X-ceptional

- Adjective: Exceptional.

- Example: "That performance was X-ceptional!"

- Cultural Note: "X-ceptional" is a playful, slangy way to describe something outstanding.

X-tra

- Adjective: Extra.

- Example: "That's x-tra braw!"

- Cultural Note: "X-tra" is used informally to emphasize something, often adding a sense of exaggeration or emphasis. The use of language in Scots is played with, and it's showcased here.

Y

Yaldi

- Exclamation: An expression of excitement or joy, similar to "hooray."

- Example: "Yaldi! We won the game!"

- Cultural Note: "Yaldi" is a term used to express excitement or joy. It's a happy and excited exclamation, often used at celebrations.

Yer

- Pronoun: Your.

- Example: "Where's yer coat?"

- Cultural Note: "Yer" is a Scottish way to say "your"

Yersel

- Pronoun: Yourself.

- Example: "Do it yersel."

- Cultural Note: "Yersel" is the Scots term for "yourself"

Yon/Yin

- Pronoun: That one.

- Example: "I like yon yin over there."

- Cultural Note: "Yon" or "Yin" is used to refer to "that one," reflecting the unique structure and vocabulary of the Scots language.

Youse

- Pronoun: You (plural).

- Example: "What are youse up to tonight?"

- Cultural Note: "Youse" is used to address a group of people, highlighting the Scots' practical approach to distinguishing between singular and plural forms of "you."

Z

Zarrafact

- Phrase: Is that a fact?

- Example: "Zarrafact? I didn't know that!"

- Cultural Note: "Zarrafact" is a humorous way to ask if something is true. It shows the Scots' capacity to play with language and to ask questions.

Zooter

- Noun: Nothing (used humorously).

- Example: "There's zooter left in the fridge."

- Cultural Note: "Zooter" is a humorous term for nothing, showcasing the playful and light-hearted aspect of the Scots language.

Scottish Idioms and Phrases

Immerse yourself in the colorful world of Scottish idioms and phrases. In this chapter, you'll find humorous sayings, timeless wisdom, and expressions that capture the Scottish spirit.

Away an bile yer heid

- Meaning: Go away and stop bothering me.
- Example: "Away an bile yer heid, I'm no' in the mood for yer nonsense!"
- Cultural Note: A blunt but funny way of telling someone to leave you alone.

Awa' wi' ye!

- Meaning: Away with you!
- Example: "Awa' wi' ye! I dinnae believe a word yer sayin'!"
- Cultural Note: Used in jest, it's a playful way of dismissing someone or something firm enough not to have a sting.

Bob's your uncle

- Meaning: There you go! Easy peasy!
- Example: "Just follow these steps and Bob's your uncle!"
- Cultural Note: "Bob's your uncle" is a phrase used to indicate that something is simple or easily done. It is a comforting phrase that is used to describe quite simple procedures.

Dinnae fash yersel

- Meaning: Don't worry yourself.
- Example: "Dinnae fash yersel, I'll take care of it."
- Cultural note: An idiom used to comfort someone. It emphasizes the Scottish value of looking out for each other.

Get yersel tae!
- Meaning: Get lost!
- Example: "Get yersel tae, I dinnae want tae see ye!"
- Cultural note: A blunt and humorous way of telling someone to leave.

Haste ye back!
- Meaning: Return soon!
- Example: "Thanks for visiting, haste ye back!"

- Cultural Note: Used as a way to say goodbye in a friendly way with the hope of seeing you quickly again.

Haud yer wheesht!
- Meaning: Be quiet!
- Example: "Haud yer wheesht, I'm tryin' tae think!"
- Cultural note: This is a playful but definite way of telling someone to stop talking. It's the Scottish way of being direct and humorous.

He's a wee nyaff
- Meaning: He's an annoying or silly person.
- Example: "Och, ignore him, he's just a wee nyaff."
- Cultural note: A fairly light-hearted way of describing someone who is a bit of a pain in the ass, in a teasing way.

Heid like a melted wellie
- Meaning: Not very clever.
- Example: "He tried to fix the sink and flooded the kitchen, heid like a melted wellie!"
- Cultural Note: Used in jest to describe someone who is not the sharpest tool in the place.

I'm awa' for a wee nap
- Meaning: I'm going for a short nap.
- Example: "I'm fair knackered, I'm awa' for a wee nap."
- Cultural note: The Scots love their "wee" (little) things, and this idiom reflects their relaxed attitude to rest.

I'm fair puckled!
- Meaning: I'm exhausted!
- Example: "After that hike, I'm fair puckled!"
- Cultural Note: It's a funny, exaggerated way of saying you're tired and is usually used playfully.

I'm fair scunnered
- Meaning: I'm fed up or annoyed.
- Example: "I'm fair scunnered wi' this rain!"
- Cultural Note: This idiom is typical of Scots who want to express their frustration with a few laughs.

I'm fair chuffed
- Meaning: I'm pleased or proud.
- Example: "I passed my exam, I'm fair chuffed!"
- Cultural note: This idiom is typical of the Scots' tendency to speak in a colorful and lively manner.

It's a dreich day
- Meaning: It's a dreary, gloomy day.
- Example: "I'm no' goin' oot, it's a dreich day!"
- Cultural Note: The colloquial term for Scotland's notoriously wet and often unpredictable weather.

It's a braw bricht moonlicht nicht
- Meaning: It's a beautifully bright moonlit night.
- Example: "Look oot the windae, it's a braw bricht moonlicht nicht!"
-Cultural Note: This is a poetic way of saying the Scots had a love of nature and could find beauty in simple things.

Keep The Heid
- Meaning: Stay calm, don't lose your temper.
- Example: "Keep the heid, we'll sort it out."
- Cultural Note: "Keep the heid" means to stay calm and composed, especially in stressful situations. It reflects the Scots' emphasis on maintaining composure and resolving issues peacefully.

Lang may yer lum reek!
- Meaning: May your chimney smoke for a long time (a traditional Scottish blessing for long life and prosperity).
- Example: "Thanks for coming, and lang may yer lum reek!"
- Cultural Note: "Lang may yer lum reek!" It is a traditional Scottish blessing meaning long life and prosperity. The warmth, home, and the staying power of success it represents.

Mind yer tongue!
- Meaning: Watch what you say!
- Example: "Mind yer tongue in front of the bairns."
- Cultural Note: "Mind yer tongue!" It is a warning to be careful with what you say.

Mony a mickle maks a muckle
- Meaning: Many small things make a big thing.
- Example: "Save a wee bit each month, mony a mickle maks a muckle."
- Cultural Note: This phrase speaks of this Scottish appreciation of thrift and thinking that small efforts can have big results.

Och aye, the noo!
- Meaning: Oh yes, now! (Often used sarcastically or dismissively).
- Example: "Och aye, the noo, as if that would happen."
- Cultural Note: "Och aye, the noo!" is an often used sarcastic phrase for something that is or seems so obvious or trivial.

Pure dead brilliant!
- Meaning: Fantastic.
- Example: "That concert was pure dead brilliant!"
- Cultural Note: "Pure dead brilliant!" A highly enthusiastic phrase to use when you are talking about something as fantastic as they come. It is a Scots way of speaking, which is expressive and enthusiastic.

She's got a face like a melted welly
- Meaning: She looks grumpy or unhappy.
- Example: "Dinnae ask her, she's got a face like a melted welly!"
- Cultural Note: The Scots are so creative with language that this idiom describes someone's mood with vivid imagery.

That's a sair fecht
- Meaning: That's a tough struggle.
- Example: "Workin' twa jobs is a sair fecht, but it'll be worth it."
- Cultural Note: This is a fitting reference to the Scots they could overcome challenges with determination.

Whit's fur ye'll no go past ye
- Meaning: What's meant for you won't pass you by.
- Example: "Dinnae worry aboot the job, whit's fur ye'll no go past ye."
- Cultural Note: This phrase is a saying that Scottish people believe in fate and destiny and use to comfort someone when things are uncertain.

We're a' Jock Tamson's bairns
- Meaning: We're all equal.
- Example: "Dinnae judge him, we're a' Jock Tamson's bairns."
- Cultural Note: This is to instill Scottish values of equality and community in people to treat each other fairly.

Whit ye sayin'?
- Meaning: What are you saying?
- Example: "Whit ye sayin'? I didnae catch that."
- Cultural Note: The Scots use this phrase in casual conversation, which is a reaction to the informal, friendly nature of the Scots.

Whit's fur ye'll no go past ye
- Meaning: What's meant for you won't pass you by.

- Example: "Dinnae worry aboot the job, whit's fur ye'll no go past ye."
- Cultural Note: This phrase is a saying that Scottish people believe in fate and destiny and use to comfort someone when things are uncertain.

We're a' Jock Tamson's bairns
- Meaning: We're all equal.
- Example: "Dinnae judge him, we're a' Jock Tamson's bairns."
- Cultural Note: This is to instill Scottish values of equality and community in people to treat each other fairly.

Yer aff yer heid!
- Meaning: You're crazy!
- Example: "Yer aff yer heid if you think that'll work."
- Cultural Note: "Yer aff yer heid!" It is used to tell someone that they are acting crazy. This is a humorous and emphatic way of saying you're disbelief or astonished.

Yer lookin' a bit peely-wally
- Meaning: You look pale and unwell.
- Example: "Yer lookin' a bit peely-wally, are ye feelin' alright?"
- Cultural Note: Something to check on someone's health in a caring, yet lighthearted way, which is how Scots are.

Ye're a right numpty
- Meaning: You're a silly or foolish person.
- Example: "Ye forgot yer keys again? Ye're a right numpty!"
- Cultural note: A slightly cheeky but affectionate way of telling someone they're being a bit daft.

Yer bum's oot the windae!
- Meaning: You're talking nonsense!
- Example: "When my friend claimed he could eat 50 haggis in one sitting, I told him, 'Yer bum's oot the windae!'"
- Cultural note: It is a Scottish idiom for exaggeration and playful banter.

Printed in Dunstable, United Kingdom